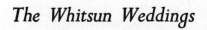

*The Whitsun Weddings*

# Books *by* Philip Larkin

## Poetry

The North Ship
The Less Deceived
The Whitsun Weddings

## Novels

Jill
A Girl in Winter

# The
# *WHITSUN*
# *WEDDINGS*

*poems by*

# Philip Larkin

*Random House*
*New York*

# Contents

# *Here*

Swerving east, from rich industrial shadows
And traffic all night north; swerving through fields
Too thin and thistled to be called meadows,
And now and then a harsh-named halt, that shields
Workmen at dawn; swerving to solitude
Of skies and scarecrows, haystacks, hares and pheasants,
And the widening river's slow presence,
The piled gold clouds, the shining gull-marked mud,

Gathers to the surprise of a large town:
Here domes and statues, spires and cranes cluster
Beside grain-scattered streets, barge-crowded water,
And residents from raw estates, brought down
The dead straight miles by stealing flat-faced trolleys,
Push through plate-glass swing doors to their desires—
Cheap suits, red kitchen-ware, sharp shoes, iced lollies,
Electric mixers, toasters, washers, driers—

A cut-price crowd, urban yet simple, dwelling
Where only salesmen and relations come
Within a terminate and fishy-smelling
Pastoral of ships up streets, the slave museum,
Tattoo-shops, consulates, grim head-scarfed wives;
And out beyond its mortgaged half-built edges
Fast-shadowed wheat-fields, running high as hedges,
Isolate villages, where removed lives

Loneliness clarifies. Here silence stands
Like heat. Here leaves unnoticed thicken,
Hidden weeds flower, neglected waters quicken,
Luminously-peopled air ascends;
And past the poppies bluish neutral distance
Ends the land suddenly beyond a beach
Of shapes and shingle. Here is unfenced existence:
Facing the sun, untalkative, out of reach.

9

# Mr Bleaney

'This was Mr Bleaney's room. He stayed
The whole time he was at the Bodies, till
They moved him.' Flowered curtains, thin and frayed,
Fall to within five inches of the sill,

Whose window shows a strip of building land,
Tussocky, littered. 'Mr Bleaney took
My bit of garden properly in hand.'
Bed, upright chair, sixty-watt bulb, no hook

Behind the door, no room for books or bags—
'I'll take it.' So it happens that I lie
Where Mr Bleaney lay, and stub my fags
On the same saucer-souvenir, and try

Stuffing my ears with cotton-wool, to drown
The jabbering set he egged her on to buy.
I know his habits—what time he came down,
His preference for sauce to gravy, why

He kept on plugging at the four aways—
Likewise their yearly frame: the Frinton folk
Who put him up for summer holidays,
And Christmas at his sister's house in Stoke.

But if he stood and watched the frigid wind
Tousling the clouds, lay on the fusty bed
Telling himself that this was home, and grinned,
And shivered, without shaking off the dread

That how we live measures our own nature,
And at his age having no more to show
Than one hired box should make him pretty sure
He warranted no better, I don't know.

# Nothing To Be Said

For nations vague as weed,
For nomads among stones,
Small-statured cross-faced tribes
And cobble-close families
In mill-towns on dark mornings
Life is slow dying.

So are their separate ways
Of building, benediction,
Measuring love and money
Ways of slow dying.
The day spent hunting pig
Or holding a garden-party,

Hours giving evidence
Or birth, advance
On death equally slowly.
And saying so to some
Means nothing; others it leaves
Nothing to be said.

# Love Songs in Age

She kept her songs, they took so little space,
  The covers pleased her:
One bleached from lying in a sunny place,
One marked in circles by a vase of water,
One mended, when a tidy fit had seized her,
  And coloured, by her daughter—
So they had waited, till in widowhood
She found them, looking for something else, and stood

Relearning how each frank submissive chord
  Had ushered in
Word after sprawling hyphenated word,
And the unfailing sense of being young
Spread out like a spring-woken tree, wherein
  That hidden freshness sung,
That certainty of time laid up in store
As when she played them first. But, even more,

The glare of that much-mentioned brilliance, love,
  Broke out, to show
Its bright incipience sailing above,
Still promising to solve, and satisfy,
And set unchangeably in order. So
  To pile them back, to cry,
Was hard, without lamely admitting how
It had not done so then, and could not now.

## Naturally the Foundation will
## Bear Your Expenses

Hurrying to catch my Comet
    One dark November day,
Which soon would snatch me from it
    To the sunshine of Bombay,
I pondered pages Berkeley
    Not three weeks since had heard,
Perceiving Chatto darkly
    Through the mirror of the Third.

Crowds, colourless and careworn,
    Had made my taxi late,
Yet not till I was airborne
    Did I recall the date—
That day when Queen and Minister
    And Band of Guards and all
Still act their solemn-sinister
    Wreath-rubbish in Whitehall.

It used to make me throw up,
    These mawkish nursery games:
O when will England grow up?
    —But I outsoar the Thames,
And dwindle off down Auster
    To greet Professor Lal
(He once met Morgan Forster),
    My contact and my pal.

# Broadcast

Giant whispering and coughing from
Vast Sunday-full and organ-frowned-on spaces
Precede a sudden scuttle on the drum,
'The Queen', and huge resettling. Then begins
A snivel on the violins:
I think of your face among all those faces,

Beautiful and devout before
Cascades of monumental slithering,
One of your gloves unnoticed on the floor
Beside those new, slightly-outmoded shoes.
Here it goes quickly dark. I lose
All but the outline of the still and withering

Leaves on half-emptied trees. Behind
The glowing wavebands, rabid storms of chording
By being distant overpower my mind
All the more shamelessly, their cut-off shout
Leaving me desperate to pick out
Your hands, tiny in all that air, applauding.

## Toads Revisited

Walking around in the park
Should feel better than work:
The lake, the sunshine,
The grass to lie on,

Blurred playground noises
Beyond black-stockinged nurses—
Not a bad place to be.
Yet it doesn't suit me,

Being one of the men
You meet of an afternoon:
Palsied old step-takers,
Hare-eyed clerks with the jitters,

Waxed-fleshed out-patients
Still vague from accidents,
And characters in long coats
Deep in the litter-baskets—

All dodging the toad work
By being stupid or weak.
Think of being them!
Hearing the hours chime,

Watching the bread delivered,
The sun by clouds covered,
The children going home;
Think of being them,

Turning over their failures
By some bed of lobelias,
Nowhere to go but indoors,
No friends but empty chairs—

## Faith Healing

Slowly the women file to where he stands
Upright in rimless glasses, silver hair,
Dark suit, white collar. Stewards tirelessly
Persuade them onwards to his voice and hands,
Within whose warm spring rain of loving care
Each dwells some twenty seconds. *Now, dear child,
What's wrong*, the deep American voice demands,
And, scarcely pausing, goes into a prayer
Directing God about this eye, that knee.
Their heads are clasped abruptly; then, exiled

Like losing thoughts, they go in silence; some
Sheepishly stray, not back into their lives
Just yet; but some stay stiff, twitching and loud
With deep hoarse tears, as if a kind of dumb
And idiot child within them still survives
To re-awake at kindness, thinking a voice
At last calls them alone, that hands have come
To lift and lighten; and such joy arrives
Their thick tongues blort, their eyes squeeze grief, a crowd
Of huge unheard answers jam and rejoice—

What's wrong! Moustached in flowered frocks they shake:
By now, all's wrong. In everyone there sleeps
A sense of life lived according to love.
To some it means the difference they could make
By loving others, but across most it sweeps
As all they might have done had they been loved.
That nothing cures. An immense slackening ache,
As when, thawing, the rigid landscape weeps,
Spreads slowly through them—that, and the voice above
Saying *Dear child*, and all time has disproved.

## For Sidney Bechet

That note you hold, narrowing and rising, shakes
Like New Orleans reflected on the water,
And in all ears appropriate falsehood wakes,

Building for some a legendary Quarter
Of balconies, flower-baskets and quadrilles,
Everyone making love and going shares—

Oh, play that thing! Mute glorious Storyvilles
Others may license, grouping round their chairs
Sporting-house girls like circus tigers (priced

Far above rubies) to pretend their fads,
While scholars *manqués* nod around unnoticed
Wrapped up in personnels like old plaids.

On me your voice falls as they say love should,
Like an enormous yes. My Crescent City
Is where your speech alone is understood,

And greeted as the natural noise of good,
Scattering long-haired grief and scored pity.

## Home is so Sad

Home is so sad. It stays as it was left,
Shaped to the comfort of the last to go
As if to win them back. Instead, bereft
Of anyone to please, it withers so,
Having no heart to put aside the theft

And turn again to what it started as,
A joyous shot at how things ought to be,
Long fallen wide. You can see how it was:
Look at the pictures and the cutlery.
The music in the piano stool. That vase.

No, give me my in-tray,
My loaf-haired secretary,
My shall-I-keep-the-call-in-Sir:
What else can I answer,

When the lights come on at four
At the end of another year?
Give me your arm, old toad;
Help me down Cemetery Road.

# Water

If I were called in
To construct a religion
I should make use of water.

Going to church
Would entail a fording
To dry, different clothes;

My litany would employ
Images of sousing,
A furious devout drench,

And I should raise in the east
A glass of water
Where any-angled light
Would congregate endlessly.

# The Whitsun Weddings

That Whitsun, I was late getting away:
   Not till about
One-twenty on the sunlit Saturday
Did my three-quarters-empty train pull out,
All windows down, all cushions hot, all sense
Of being in a hurry gone. We ran
Behind the backs of houses, crossed a street
Of blinding windscreens, smelt the fish-dock; thence
The river's level drifting breadth began,
Where sky and Lincolnshire and water meet.

All afternoon, through the tall heat that slept
   For miles inland,
A slow and stopping curve southwards we kept.
Wide farms went by, short-shadowed cattle, and
Canals with floatings of industrial froth;
A hothouse flashed uniquely: hedges dipped
And rose: and now and then a smell of grass
Displaced the reek of buttoned carriage-cloth
Until the next town, new and nondescript,
Approached with acres of dismantled cars.

At first, I didn't notice what a noise
   The weddings made
Each station that we stopped at: sun destroys
The interest of what's happening in the shade,
And down the long cool platforms whoops and skirls
I took for porters larking with the mails,
And went on reading. Once we started, though,
We passed them, grinning and pomaded, girls
In parodies of fashion, heels and veils,
All posed irresolutely, watching us go,

As if out on the end of an event
   Waving goodbye
To something that survived it. Struck, I leant
More promptly out next time, more curiously,
And saw it all again in different terms:
The fathers with broad belts under their suits
And seamy foreheads; mothers loud and fat;
An uncle shouting smut; and then the perms,
The nylon gloves and jewellery-substitutes,
The lemons, mauves, and olive-ochres that

Marked off the girls unreally from the rest.
   Yes, from cafés
And banquet-halls up yards, and bunting-dressed
Coach-party annexes, the wedding-days
Were coming to an end. All down the line
Fresh couples climbed aboard: the rest stood round;
The last confetti and advice were thrown,
And, as we moved, each face seemed to define
Just what it saw departing: children frowned
At something dull; fathers had never known

Success so huge and wholly farcical;
   The women shared
The secret like a happy funeral;
While girls, gripping their handbags tighter, stared
At a religious wounding. Free at last,
And loaded with the sum of all they saw,
We hurried towards London, shuffling gouts of steam.
Now fields were building-plots, and poplars cast
Long shadows over major roads, and for
Some fifty minutes, that in time would seem

Just long enough to settle hats and say
   *I nearly died*,
A dozen marriages got under way.
They watched the landscape, sitting side by side
—An Odeon went past, a cooling tower,

And someone running up to bowl—and none
Thought of the others they would never meet
Or how their lives would all contain this hour.
I thought of London spread out in the sun,
Its postal districts packed like squares of wheat:

There we were aimed. And as we raced across
   Bright knots of rail
Past standing Pullmans, walls of blackened moss
Came close, and it was nearly done, this frail
Travelling coincidence; and what it held
Stood ready to be loosed with all the power
That being changed can give. We slowed again,
And as the tightened brakes took hold, there swelled
A sense of falling, like an arrow-shower
Sent out of sight, somewhere becoming rain.

# Self's the Man

Oh, no one can deny
That Arnold is less selfish than I.
He married a woman to stop her getting away
Now she's there all day,

And the money he gets for wasting his life on work
She takes as her perk
To pay for the kiddies' clobber and the drier
And the electric fire,

And when he finishes supper
Planning to have a read at the evening paper
It's *Put a screw in this wall*—
He has no time at all,

With the nippers to wheel round the houses
And the hall to paint in his old trousers
And that letter to her mother
Saying *Won't you come for the summer.*

To compare his life and mine
Makes me feel a swine:
Oh, no one can deny
That Arnold is less selfish than I.

But wait, not so fast:
Is there such a contrast?
He was out for his own ends
Not just pleasing his friends;

And if it was such a mistake
He still did it for his own sake,
Playing his own game.
So he and I are the same,

Only I'm a better hand
At knowing what I can stand
Without them sending a van—
Or I suppose I can.

# Take One Home for the Kiddies

On shallow straw, in shadeless glass,
Huddled by empty bowls, they sleep:
No dark, no dam, no earth, no grass—
*Mam, get us one of them to keep.*

Living toys are something novel,
But it soon wears off somehow.
Fetch the shoebox, fetch the shovel—
*Mam, we're playing funerals now.*

# Days

What are days for?
Days are where we live.
They come, they wake us
Time and time over.
They are to be happy in:
Where can we live but days?

Ah, solving that question
Brings the priest and the doctor
In their long coats
Running over the fields.

# MCMXIV

Those long uneven lines
Standing as patiently
As if they were stretched outside
The Oval or Villa Park,
The crowns of hats, the sun
On moustached archaic faces
Grinning as if it were all
An August Bank Holiday lark;

And the shut shops, the bleached
Established names on the sunblinds,
The farthings and sovereigns,
And dark-clothed children at play
Called after kings and queens,
The tin advertisements
For cocoa and twist, and the pubs
Wide open all day;

And the countryside not caring:
The place-names all hazed over
With flowering grasses, and fields
Shadowing Domesday lines
Under wheat's restless silence;
The differently-dressed servants
With tiny rooms in huge houses,
The dust behind limousines;

Never such innocence,
Never before or since,
As changed itself to past
Without a word—the men
Leaving the gardens tidy,
The thousands of marriages
Lasting a little while longer:
Never such innocence again.

# Talking in Bed

Talking in bed ought to be easiest,
Lying together there goes back so far,
An emblem of two people being honest.

Yet more and more time passes silently.
Outside, the wind's incomplete unrest
Builds and disperses clouds about the sky,

And dark towns heap up on the horizon.
None of this cares for us. Nothing shows why
At this unique distance from isolation

It becomes still more difficult to find
Words at once true and kind,
Or not untrue and not unkind.

# The Large Cool Store

The large cool store selling cheap clothes
Set out in simple sizes plainly
(Knitwear, Summer Casuals, Hose,
In browns and greys, maroon and navy)
Conjures the weekday world of those

Who leave at dawn low terraced houses
Timed for factory, yard and site.
But past the heaps of shirts and trousers
Spread the stands of Modes For Night:
Machine-embroidered, thin as blouses,

Lemon, sapphire, moss-green, rose
Bri-Nylon Baby-Dolls and Shorties
Flounce in clusters. To suppose
They share that world, to think their sort is
Matched by something in it, shows

How separate and unearthly love is,
Or women are, or what they do,
Or in our young unreal wishes
Seem to be: synthetic, new,
And natureless in ecstasies.

# A Study of Reading Habits

When getting my nose in a book
Cured most things short of school,
It was worth ruining my eyes
To know I could still keep cool,
And deal out the old right hook
To dirty dogs twice my size.

Later, with inch-thick specs,
Evil was just my lark:
Me and my cloak and fangs
Had ripping times in the dark.
The women I clubbed with sex!
I broke them up like meringues.

Don't read much now: the dude
Who lets the girl down before
The hero arrives, the chap
Who's yellow and keeps the store,
Seem far too familiar. Get stewed:
Books are a load of crap.

# The Importance of Elsewhere

Lonely in Ireland, since it was not home,
Strangeness made sense. The salt rebuff of speech,
Insisting so on difference, made me welcome:
Once that was recognised, we were in touch.

Their draughty streets, end-on to hills, the faint
Archaic smell of dockland, like a stable,
The herring-hawker's cry, dwindling, went
To prove me separate, not unworkable.

Living in England has no such excuse:
These are my customs and establishments
It would be much more serious to refuse.
Here no elsewhere underwrites my existence.

# Sunny Prestatyn

Come To Sunny Prestatyn
Laughed the girl on the poster,
Kneeling up on the sand
In tautened white satin.
Behind her, a hunk of coast, a
Hotel with palms
Seemed to expand from her thighs and
Spread breast-lifting arms.

She was slapped up one day in March.
A couple of weeks, and her face
Was snaggle-toothed and boss-eyed;
Huge tits and a fissured crotch
Were scored well in, and the space
Between her legs held scrawls
That set her fairly astride
A tuberous cock and balls

Autographed *Titch Thomas*, while
Someone had used a knife
Or something to stab right through
The moustached lips of her smile.
She was too good for this life.
Very soon, a great transverse tear
Left only a hand and some blue.
Now *Fight Cancer* is there.

# First Sight

Lambs that learn to walk in snow
When their bleating clouds the air
Meet a vast unwelcome, know
Nothing but a sunless glare.
Newly stumbling to and fro
All they find, outside the fold,
Is a wretched width of cold.

As they wait beside the ewe,
Her fleeces wetly caked, there lies
Hidden round them, waiting too,
Earth's immeasurable surprise.
They could not grasp it if they knew,
What so soon will wake and grow
Utterly unlike the snow.

# Dockery and Son

'Dockery was junior to you,
Wasn't he?' said the Dean. 'His son's here now.'
Death-suited, visitant, I nod. 'And do
You keep in touch with——' Or remember how
Black-gowned, unbreakfasted, and still half-tight
We used to stand before that desk, to give
'Our version' of 'these incidents last night'?
I try the door of where I used to live:

Locked. The lawn spreads dazzlingly wide.
A known bell chimes. I catch my train, ignored.
Canal and clouds and colleges subside
Slowly from view. But Dockery, good Lord,
Anyone up today must have been born
In '43, when I was twenty-one.
If he was younger, did he get this son
At nineteen, twenty? Was he that withdrawn

High-collared public-schoolboy, sharing rooms
With Cartwright who was killed? Well, it just shows
How much . . . How little . . . Yawning, I suppose
I fell asleep, waking at the fumes
And furnace-glares of Sheffield, where I changed,
And ate an awful pie, and walked along
The platform to its end to see the ranged
Joining and parting lines reflect a strong

Unhindered moon. To have no son, no wife,
No house or land still seemed quite natural.
Only a numbness registered the shock
Of finding out how much had gone of life,
How widely from the others. Dockery, now:
Only nineteen, he must have taken stock
Of what he wanted, and been capable
Of . . . No, that's not the difference: rather, how

Convinced he was he should be added to!
Why did he think adding meant increase?
To me it was dilution. Where do these
Innate assumptions come from? Not from what
We think truest, or most want to do:
Those warp tight-shut, like doors. They're more a style
Our lives bring with them: habit for a while,
Suddenly they harden into all we've got

And how we got it; looked back on, they rear
Like sand-clouds, thick and close, embodying
For Dockery a son, for me nothing,
Nothing with all a son's harsh patronage.
Life is first boredom, then fear.
Whether or not we use it, it goes,
And leaves what something hidden from us chose,
And age, and then the only end of age.

# Ignorance

Strange to know nothing, never to be sure
Of what is true or right or real,
But forced to qualify *or so I feel*,
Or *Well, it does seem so:*
*Someone must know.*

Strange to be ignorant of the way things work:
Their skill at finding what they need,
Their sense of shape, and punctual spread of seed,
And willingness to change;
Yes, it is strange,

Even to wear such knowledge—for our flesh
Surrounds us with its own decisions—
And yet spend all our life on imprecisions,
That when we start to die
Have no idea why.

# Reference Back

*That was a pretty one*, I heard you call
From the unsatisfactory hall
To the unsatisfactory room where I
Played record after record, idly,
Wasting my time at home, that you
Looked so much forward to.

Oliver's *Riverside Blues*, it was. And now
I shall, I suppose, always remember how
The flock of notes those antique negroes blew
Out of Chicago air into
A huge remembering pre-electric horn
The year after I was born
Three decades later made this sudden bridge
From your unsatisfactory age
To my unsatisfactory prime.

Truly, though our element is time,
We are not suited to the long perspectives
Open at each instant of our lives.
They link us to our losses: worse,
They show us what we have as it once was,
Blindingly undiminished, just as though
By acting differently we could have kept it so.

# Wild Oats

About twenty years ago
Two girls came in where I worked—
A bosomy English rose
And her friend in specs I could talk to.
Faces in those days sparked
The whole shooting-match off, and I doubt
If ever one had like hers:
But it was the friend I took out,

And in seven years after that
Wrote over four hundred letters,
Gave a ten-guinea ring
I got back in the end, and met
At numerous cathedral cities
Unknown to the clergy. I believe
I met beautiful twice. She was trying
Both times (so I thought) not to laugh.

Parting, after about five
Rehearsals, was an agreement
That I was too selfish, withdrawn,
And easily bored to love.
Well, useful to get that learnt.
In my wallet are still two snaps
Of bosomy rose with fur gloves on.
Unlucky charms, perhaps.

# Essential Beauty

In frames as large as rooms that face all ways
And block the ends of streets with giant loaves,
Screen graves with custard, cover slums with praise
Of motor-oil and cuts of salmon, shine
Perpetually these sharply-pictured groves
Of how life should be. High above the gutter
A silver knife sinks into golden butter,
A glass of milk stands in a meadow, and
Well-balanced families, in fine
Midsummer weather, owe their smiles, their cars,
Even their youth, to that small cube each hand
Stretches towards. These, and the deep armchairs
Aligned to cups at bedtime, radiant bars
(Gas or electric), quarter-profile cats
By slippers on warm mats,
Reflect none of the rained-on streets and squares

They dominate outdoors. Rather, they rise
Serenely to proclaim pure crust, pure foam,
Pure coldness to our live imperfect eyes
That stare beyond this world, where nothing's made
As new or washed quite clean, seeking the home
All such inhabit. There, dark raftered pubs
Are filled with white-clothed ones from tennis-clubs,
And the boy puking his heart out in the Gents
Just missed them, as the pensioner paid
A halfpenny more for Granny Graveclothes' Tea
To taste old age, and dying smokers sense
Walking towards them through some dappled park
As if on water that unfocused she
No match lit up, nor drag ever brought near,
Who now stands newly clear,
Smiling, and recognising, and going dark.

## Send No Money

Standing under the fobbed
Impendent belly of Time
*Tell me the truth*, I said,
*Teach me the way things go.*
All the other lads there
Were itching to have a bash,
But I thought wanting unfair:
It and finding out clash.

So he patted my head, booming *Boy,*
*There's no green in your eye:*
*Sit here, and watch the hail*
*Of occurrence clobber life out*
*To a shape no one sees—*
*Dare you look at that straight?*
*Oh thank you*, I said, *Oh yes please,*
And sat down to wait.

Half life is over now,
And I meet full face on dark mornings
The bestial visor, bent in
By the blows of what happened to happen.
What does it prove? Sod all.
In this way I spent youth,
Tracing the trite untransferable
Truss-advertisement, truth.

# Afternoons

Summer is fading:
The leaves fall in ones and twos
From trees bordering
The new recreation ground.
In the hollows of afternoons
Young mothers assemble
At swing and sandpit
Setting free their children.

Behind them, at intervals,
Stand husbands in skilled trades,
An estateful of washing,
And the albums, lettered
*Our Wedding*, lying
Near the television:
Before them, the wind
Is ruining their courting-places

That are still courting-places
(But the lovers are all in school),
And their children, so intent on
Finding more unripe acorns,
Expect to be taken home.
Their beauty has thickened.
Something is pushing them
To the side of their own lives.

# An Arundel Tomb

Side by side, their faces blurred,
The earl and countess lie in stone,
Their proper habits vaguely shown
As jointed armour, stiffened pleat,
And that faint hint of the absurd—
The little dogs under their feet.

Such plainness of the pre-baroque
Hardly involves the eye, until
It meets his left-hand gauntlet, still
Clasped empty in the other; and
One sees, with a sharp tender shock,
His hand withdrawn, holding her hand.

They would not think to lie so long.
Such faithfulness in effigy
Was just a detail friends would see:
A sculptor's sweet commissioned grace
Thrown off in helping to prolong
The Latin names around the base.

They would not guess how early in
Their supine stationary voyage
The air would change to soundless damage,
Turn the old tenantry away;
How soon succeeding eyes begin
To look, not read. Rigidly they

Persisted, linked, through lengths and breadths
Of time. Snow fell, undated. Light
Each summer thronged the glass. A bright
Litter of birdcalls strewed the same
Bone-riddled ground. And up the paths
The endless altered people came,

Washing at their identity.
Now, helpless in the hollow of
An unarmorial age, a trough
Of smoke in slow suspended skeins
Above their scrap of history,
Only an attitude remains:

Time has transfigured them into
Untruth. The stone fidelity
They hardly meant has come to be
Their final blazon, and to prove
Our almost-instinct almost true:
What will survive of us is love.